D1123225

Nature-Inspired Innovations

Biomimic
BUILDING

Before Reading:

Building Academic Vocabulary and Background Knowledge

Before reading a book, it is important to tap into what your child or students already know about the topic. This will help them develop their vocabulary, increase their reading comprehension, and make connections across the curriculum.

1. *Look at the cover of the book. What will this book be about?*
2. *What do you already know about the topic?*
3. *Let's study the Table of Contents. What will you learn about in the book's chapters?*
4. *What would you like to learn about this topic? Do you think you might learn about it from this book? Why or why not?*
5. *Use a reading journal to write about your knowledge of this topic. Record what you already know about the topic and what you hope to learn about the topic.*
6. *Read the book.*
7. *In your reading journal, record what you learned about the topic and your response to the book.*
8. *After reading the book complete the activities below.*

Content Area Vocabulary

Read the list. What do these words mean?

biomimicry
biomineralization
biomorphic
carbon dioxide
exoskeleton
hydrophilic
hydrophobic
porous
pyramidal
resilient
turbines

After Reading:

Comprehension and Extension Activity

After reading the book, work on the following questions with your child or students in order to check their level of reading comprehension and content mastery.

1. *What ways do building designers and engineers mimic nature? (Summarize)*
2. *What does a tree do to survive and grow that has inspired biomimicry in building? (Asking questions)*
3. *What kind of house would you build that mimicked the way nature survives? (Text to self connection)*
4. *How can biomimicry in building help reduce CO2 emissions? (Asking questions)*
5. *Why is inspiration from nature a good way to create new kinds of building products and structures? (infer)*

Extension Activity

Building designers are often inspired by nature. From this list of animals, think of something they do that inspired an idea for a builder: desert beetle, bird, sea sponge, termite, mussel.

Table of Contents

Introduction

Spookfish live deep in the ocean where there is very little light. Spookfish have specialized eyes that work as mirrors to help them to see.

Its eyes are split so that one half points up toward daylight and the other points down to the dark ocean depths. This feature allows the fish to pick up low levels of light. The mirrors aim the light down where possible meals are swimming by.

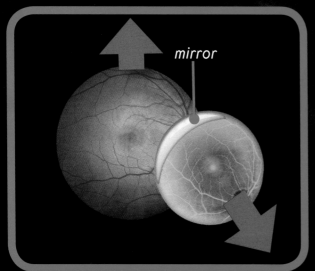

mirror

A spookfish's down-facing eyes use mirrors instead of lenses, with hundreds of tiny crystals collecting and focusing light.

brownsnout spookfish
© OCEANA

Looking up into the Atrium of the Fulton Center, New York

Architects have created buildings that use a similar method of bringing daylight into darkness. The Fulton Center is an underground subway station and shopping center. Its designers created a skylight surrounded by a net of stainless steel cables and aluminum panels. The unique arrangement of the panels works to distribute beams of light throughout the day to the ground below. The Fulton Center is an example of **biomimicry** in building.

Biomimicry, also called biomimetics, involves the study of how functions are delivered in biology, then translating those functions into designs that suit human needs. Architects, scientists, and engineers involved in biomimicry have recognized that nature is the world's largest science and engineering lab.

The designers deliberately mimicked the structure of a bird's nest for the Beijing National Stadium. They felt that a nest would embrace and nurture the people inside.

Nature has 3.8 billion years of experience! Using nature as an inspiration and guide, biomimics research, experiment with, and create innovative designs that help solve human problems. Nature-inspired building designs, materials, and systems can provide better ways for people to thrive in their environments.

The Harpa concert hall in Iceland was inspired by the island country's basalt rock formations. Inside, the concert halls mimic other natural elements found in Iceland.

Biomimicry in Design and Energy Conservation

The Fulton Center is just one example of biology-inspired building design. The unique shading techniques of the durian fruit inspired the design for the Esplanade Theaters in Singapore.

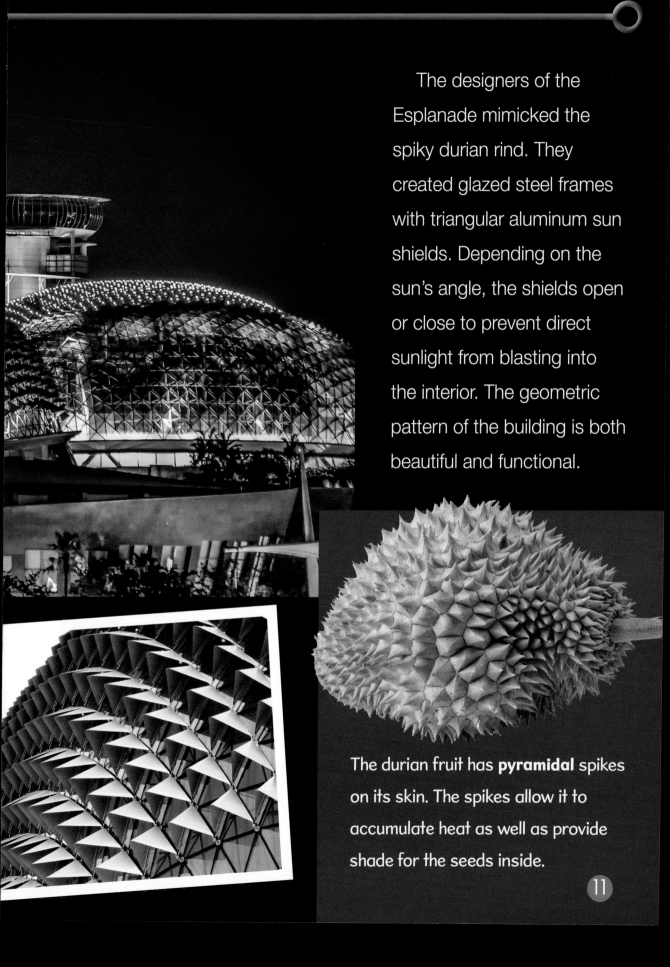

The designers of the Esplanade mimicked the spiky durian rind. They created glazed steel frames with triangular aluminum sun shields. Depending on the sun's angle, the shields open or close to prevent direct sunlight from blasting into the interior. The geometric pattern of the building is both beautiful and functional.

The durian fruit has **pyramidal** spikes on its skin. The spikes allow it to accumulate heat as well as provide shade for the seeds inside.

A professor at the University of Warwick's School of Engineering spent many years studying the forms and shapes in nature. She wanted to understand how they could easily withstand natural forces. By studying natural objects, the professor came up with a new way to build a bridge.

The professor used a process called form-finding to create a structural design that can withstand the stress of severe weather and traffic. She mimicked the way a leaf can deal with being whipped around by the forces of nature. Using form-finding, a rigid structure is designed to follow a natural form. It relies on compression for its strength. The design would give the bridge the ability to survive repeated or severe loading forces that damage or destroy more conventional designs.

Millennium Bridg

Form-finding is finding the natural form, often inspired by nature, that gives a structure more strength. Another example of form-finding is the Gateshead Millennium Bridge in the UK. The designers modeled it after the form and function of an eyelid. When the "lid" closes, people can move across it. When the lid opens, ships can pass underneath.

A darkling beetle of the Namib Desert knows how to get a drink of water in the dry desert. The beetle has bumps on its back that are **hydrophilic**, or water-loving. Waxy areas between the bumps are **hydrophobic**, or water-fearing.

darkling beetle

During the night, the ocean fog travels over the beetle's back. Water droplets accumulate on the bumps. When the beetle lifts up its rear, the droplets roll down a waxy channel and into the beetle's mouth! The beetle gets a drink, then heads back into hiding before the sun comes up.

The Namib Desert is a vast, arid desert that stretches from the Atlantic Ocean into parts of Namibia, Angola, and South Africa. The desert temperatures can rise to 140° Fahrenheit (60°C) during the day and down to 32° Fahrenheit (0°C) at night.

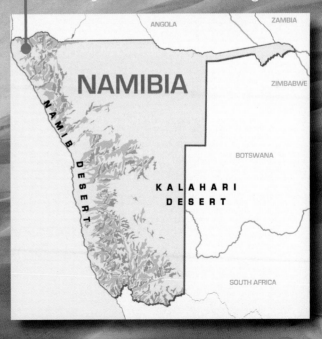

ANGOLA

ZAMBIA

NAMIBIA

ZIMBABWE

NAMIB DESERT

BOTSWANA

KALAHARI
DESERT

SOUTH AFRICA

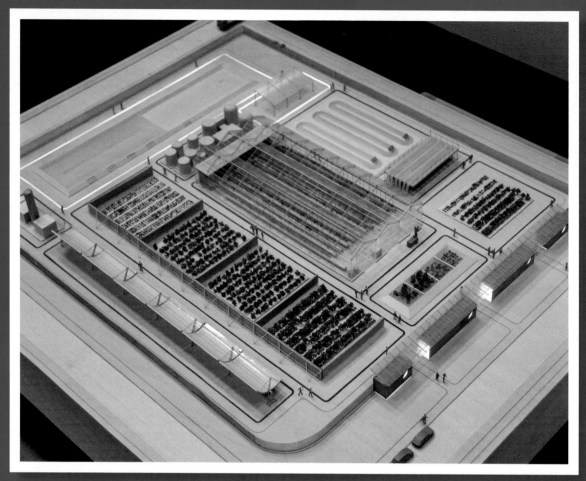

Miniature model of the Sahara Forest Project's pilot facility in Qatar

Architect Michael Pawlyn based the design of the seawater-cooled greenhouse for the Sahara Forest Project on the way this beetle collects water. Moisture on the greenhouse condenses humidity into freshwater much like the back of the darkling beetle.

The system produced enough water for the plants inside the greenhouse. There was excess water to spread on the surrounding area. The desert around the greenhouse turned from formerly barren land into a green area, all thanks to mimicking a tiny beetle.

The Gherkin, a tower in the UK, has an air ventilation system that was nature-inspired. Its skin structure is based on a sea sponge called the Venus's flower basket.. The sponge's **exoskeleton** helps to disperse strong water currents while it filters water from food. Using a similar design, The Gherkin directs wind along its spiral shape. This design naturally cools the building and saves energy.

Venus's Flower Basket

The Gherkin

Sea sponges also inspired the Pearl River Tower in China. Sponges can pump thousands of gallons of water a day through their skin. The 71-story Pearl River Tower's south side is **porous** like a sponge. Wind **turbines** are housed in four holes, harvesting the wind into energy-producing turbines.

Sea sponges are multi-celled animals, not plants. Sponges use their filter feeders that are able to eat particulates both large and small. Sponges attach themselves to solid surfaces where hopefully food is abundant.

Pearl River Tower

termite mound

The Eastgate Center in Harare, Zimbabwe, was inspired by the gigantic mounds constructed by African termites. The mounds are heated and cooled during the day and night through an elaborate system of vents. Air is brought in from the lower part of the mound, through muddy enclosures where the air is cooler, then up through another channel to the top.

Eastgate Center

The termites regulate the temperature by constantly creating new vents and blocking old ones. Their life quest is to keep their gardens of edible fungus alive. Then the colony is well fed, secure, and self-sufficient.

Architect Mick Pearce designed a ventilation system for the Eastgate Center that operates in a similar way. Outside air is warmed or cooled. Then it is vented into the floors and offices before it flows out of chimneys.

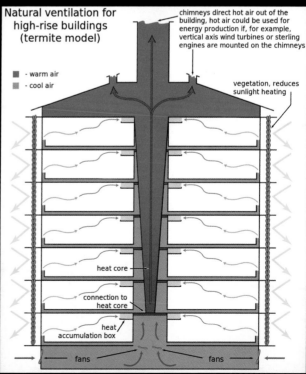

Natural ventilation for high-rise buildings (termite model)

chimneys direct hot air out of the building, hot air could be used for energy production if, for example, vertical axis wind turbines or sterling engines are mounted on the chimneys

■ - warm air
■ - cool air

vegetation, reduces sunlight heating

heat core

connection to heat core

heat accumulation box

fans   fans

Biomorphic design is the art of copying natural forms for a symbolic effect, not for its function. The Sagrada Familia cathedral is an example. The cathedral's interior design was inspired by the idea that a forest invites prayer.

Sagrada Familia cathedral

Eden was being built on top of a clay pit that was still being mined. That meant the structures needed to tolerate an uneven and shifting foundation. So, the designers at Grimshaw Architects built massive, flexible bubble domes.

Nature-Inspired Building Materials

Metal in a corrosive environment can develop corrosion fatigue. The metal slowly degrades because of corrosion and loading stress, causing it to eventually fail.

The natural world is filled with successful species of all kinds. They have survived for billions of years because of their bodily structures. Biomimics learn from nature to create materials for building that are strong, **resilient**, and hopefully, sustainable and recyclable.

Engineers depend on structural steel to be a strong and dependable building material. But that's not always true. Metal "fatigue" is often the result of spreading cracks in the metal. The cracks form because of stress and other factors. Metal fatigue has been blamed for countless structural failures. Many of those failures resulted in devastating tragedy.

Biomimics started looking at vertebrate bones for a new way to manufacture metal. A bone is a three-part structure. There is a spongy interior wrapped in dense material that is covered in connective tissue.

If a bone cracks, the crack can't spread easily through the layered structure. Thanks to biomimicry, a new kind of steel is being developed. Its layered structure is similar to a bone, and will prevent cracks from spreading.

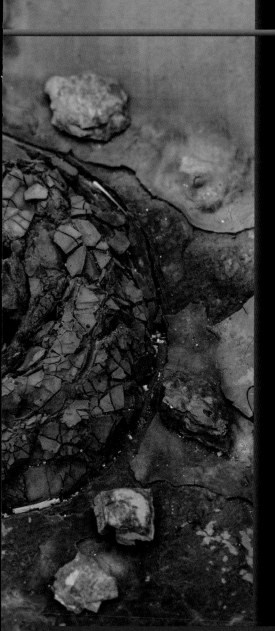

Bone Anatomy

cartilage

spongy bone

compact bone

Engineers are also inspired by the outer peel structure of a pomelo fruit. They think it might be a way to create stronger aluminum material. A pomelo is similar to a grapefruit, yet is tough enough to fall more than 30 feet (9.1 meters) without harming the tender pulp inside.

pomelo fruit

Concrete is the most widely used building material in the world. Sadly, the production of cement, a primary component, introduces massive amounts of **carbon dioxide** (CO_2) into the atmosphere. Researchers have been studying cement's natural alternative: coral.

Cement is the key component in concrete products. It is mixed with sand, crushed stone, and water to create a strong building product for just about anything. There are a variety of concrete mixes that are designed for different tasks. For buildings, concrete is always reinforced with steel bars.

Cement and concrete production is the third largest industrial source of pollution. The process creates other air-pollutant emissions besides CO_2.

The formation of coral in the oceans uses a process called **biomineralization**. Biomineralization calcifies carbon with minerals rather than releasing it into the air.

A company called Blue Planet is successfully producing cement using a process similar to coral biomineralization. They collect CO_2 from smoke stacks at a power plant. Then they run it through saltwater from the sea. The seawater has all the minerals that coral uses to calcify CO_2. This means that far less pollutants are released in the process.

A mussel is a shelled sea creature that can glue itself to almost any solid surface. Mussels secrete a protein that allows them to stick and stay in spite of constant crashing waves or other forces.

Mussels inspired a new kind of plywood glue. Plywood consists of layers of thin wood that are glued and pressed together. Kaichang Li, an Oregon State University professor, conducted the research that led to the creation of a natural adhesive for manufacturing plywood.

plywood

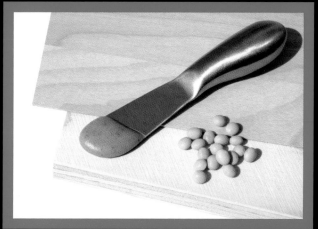

Called PureBond, the glue uses soy proteins similar to mussel secretions. This bio-adhesive is a safer alternative to the synthetic glues that are normally used for plywood and other products.

NATURE SAFETY:

Woodpecker beaks could potentially lead to better shock-absorbing helmets, earthquake-resistant buildings, and more focused and efficient jackhammers for construction workers.

Biomimicry Systems in Living Buildings

Living buildings mimic many of nature's design solutions. The goal is to make the best use of available resources and create a healthy environment. With nature as inspiration, living buildings generate and conserve energy from nontoxic resources. They also capture and treat water and strive to deal with waste. Living buildings include houses, workplaces, and even entire communities!

Vertical Forest (Bosco Verticale) in Milan, Italy, is an example of urban biomimicry that uses biodiversity to create a natural ecosystem in a crowded city.

The idea is to design living and working spaces that mimic natural ways to collect and conserve energy and water, gather nutrients, compost waste, and grow to be a healthy and successful living system.

The BIQ in Hamburg, Germany, is a structure with plants called algae growing on the sides of the building that face the sun. The algae grow and spread inside an outer shell. The algae provide insulation, control the amount of light coming in, and produce bio-gas, which is used to power the building. The BIQ is the first algae powered building in the world. It is a model for other new buildings that want to provide clean energy.

BIQ building in Hamburg, Germany

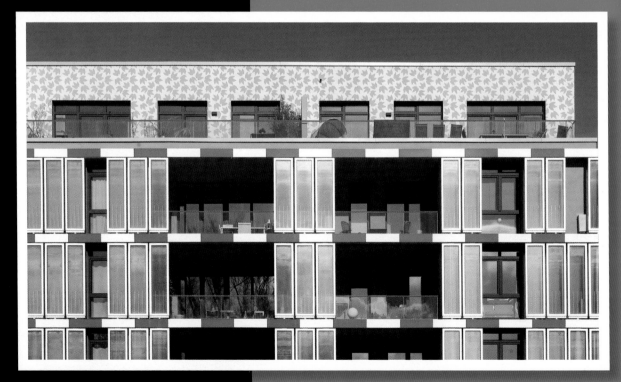

The Bullitt Center in Seattle, Washington, behaves much like a tree. Solar cells on the roof collect the sun's energy, as do leaves in a tree. And like a tree, the building has systems that collect and store rainwater.

The center also has closed-loop heat pumps that mine natural geothermal energy directly from the ground. From there, a heating system transports water through a series of tubes in the concrete floors.

The process is similar to the way a tree gathers water and nutrients from the soil. Biomimicry was a huge influence in the design and engineering for the commercial living building.

Bullitt Center, Seattle

The 1,667 foot (508 meter) skyscraper called Taipei 101 was modeled after bamboo, a giant, woody grass native to the rainforests of Southeast Asia and Africa. The eight segments of the 101-story structure each have eight floors, mimicking the segments of bamboo. The building uses a natural cooling system supplied with ice. The roof and wall water recycling systems provide much of the building's water needs. Taipei 101 holds the "World's Tallest Green Building" award for its green energy systems.

bamboo

Taipei 101, Taiwan

The eight segments of Taipei 101 represent a lucky number in Chinese culture.

Researchers and innovators continue to study and learn from nature. They discover new ways to mimic nature's brilliance, employing biomimicry for building materials, structures, and systems.

They never stop learning from and mimicking how nature has survived and thrived for billions of years. Hopefully, all buildings can be designed so that they are more efficient, sustainable, safe, healthy, and beautiful places to live. That's what has always worked for nature!

Santiago Calatrava designed a sun screen for the Milwaukee Art Museum that spans 217 feet (66 meters). Inspired by the wings of a bird, the steel screen opens up to shade the entrance during the day. It closes like folding wings at night. The wings also close automatically if there are strong winds.

WHAT WOULD YOU BUILD?

Designers and engineers use biomimicry to come up with safer, more sustainable, and more energy-efficient buildings. Choose from the list of animals on page 45 and find out where and how they live by reading about them in books or on the Internet. Design a structure for people that is inspired by one or more things your chosen animal uses for shelter. Draw your design and label the parts and what they do.

Sociable weavers build a massive nest for their entire colony.

naked mole rat

paper wasp

bushy-tailed woodrat

barn swallow

sociable weaver

beaver

Glossary

biomimicry (bye-oh-MIM-ik-ree): mimicking nature for solutions to human challenges

biomineralization (bye-oh-min-ur-uhl-uh-ZAY-shuhn): the process organisms use to produce minerals

biomorphic (bye-oh-MORF-ik): designed to mimic the shape of a living organism

CO_2 - carbon dioxide (KAR-buhn dye-OK-side): a gas that is a mixture of carbon and oxygen

exoskeleton (eks-oh-SKEL-uht-uhn): a bony structure on the outside of an animal

hydrophilic (HYE-droh-FIL-ik): will mix with or dissolve in water

hydrophobic (HYE-droh-FOH-bik): will repel or fail to mix with water

porous (POR-uhss): something that is full of tiny holes and lets liquid or gas through it

pyramidal (PIRH-uh-mid-uhl): shaped like a polygon that has a base and triangular sides that meet at a point on top

resilient (rih-ZI-li-uhnt): able to resume shape after being pressed or stretched

turbines (TUR-bines): engines driven by water, steam, or gas passing through the blades of a wheel and making it revolve

Index

Show What You Know

1. What is the difference between biomimicry and biomorphism in building design?
2. What is one example of how nature has inspired energy conservation in building?
3. What is one example of a building material inspired by nature?
4. What kinds of building ideas did termites give to designers?
5. Why would a structure be inspired by a soap bubble?

Further Reading

Beck, Barbara, *The Future Architect's Tool Kit*, Schiffer, 2016.

Koontz, Robin, *Think Like an Engineer*, Rourke Educational Media, 2017.

Vorderman, Carol, *How to Be an Engineer*, DK Children, 2018.

About the Author

Robin Koontz is a freelance author/illustrator of a wide variety of nonfiction and fiction books, educational blogs, and magazine articles for children and young adults. Her 2011 science title, *Leaps and Creeps - How Animals Move to Survive*, was an Animal Behavior Society Outstanding Children's Book Award Finalist. Raised in Maryland and Alabama, Robin now lives with her husband in the Coast Range of western Oregon where she especially enjoys observing the wildlife on her property. You can learn more on her blog: robinkoontz. wordpress.com.

Meet The Author!
www.meetREMauthors.com

www.rourkeeducationalmedia.com

PHOTO CREDITS: Cover: singapore opera house © Kisov Boris, bubbles © Lolinda, eden © Edith Rum, durian fruit skin © By panda3800; page 6 © Fotos593; page 7 © SIHASAKPRACHUM, inset photo © Eastimages; page 8-9 Harpa Building © KeongDaGreat, landscape with ocean © Felix Lipov, landscape closeup © George Koultouridis; page 10-11 opera house © Juriah Mosin, fruit closeup © antpkr, durian fruit © Atwood, building closeup © Jordan Tan; page 12-13 © ColourArt; page 14-15 desert/ocean © Radek Borovka, beetle © Ajmal Thaha, map © Pjasha; page 17 gherkin building © Milind Arvind Ketkar, page 17 venus flower basket sponge © Dmitry Grigoriev, page 18-19 Pearl River Tower © GuoZhongHua, ocean image © Stubblefield Photography, page 20-21 termite mound © EcoPrint; page 22-23 cathedral © TTstudio, cathedral interior © William Perugini; page 24-25 bubbles © Khomulo Anna, interior of building with plants © David Quixley, buildings © mambo6435, page 26-27 © Dr Morley Read; page 28-29 © Kimtaro, page 28 bone illustration © Alila Medical Media, page 29 © Atwood; page 30-31 cityscape © Wang An Qi, page 31 smoke stacks © Jeff Zehnder, page 32-33 coral © John Cuyos; page 34-35 mussels © aurelie le moigne, page 35 plywood © Noppharat4969; page 35 woodpecker © Mircea Costina, page 36-37 © faber1893; page 38 BIQ house © ricochet64; page 40-41 © ESB Professional, bamboo © leungchopan; page 42-43 © Keya5, inset photo © Sue Stokes; page 44-45 barn swallow © Super Prin, beaver © Jody Ann, sociable weaver © Johan Swanepoel, weaver nest © Adwo, naked mole rat © Neil Bromhall, paper wasp © Dave Montreuil
All photos from Shutterstock.com except: pages 4-5 snookfish © OCEANA; page 16 courtesy of The Sahara Forest Project; page 20-21 Eastgate Center photo: Wikipedia https://creativecommons.org/licenses/by-sa/3.0/deed.en, illustration by Fred the Oyster https://creativecommons.org/licenses/by-sa/3.0/deed.en; page 39 © Joe Mabel https://creativecommons.org/licenses/by-sa/3.0/deed.en; page 45 bushy tailed woodrat courtesy of U.S. Department of Agriculture

Edited by: Keli Sipperley

Produced by Blue Door Education for Rourke Educational Media. Cover and Interior design by: Nicola Stratford   www.nicolastratford.com

Library of Congress PCN Data

Biomimic Building / Robin Koontz
(Nature-Inspired Innovations)
ISBN 978-1-64156-454-0 (hard cover)
ISBN 978-1-64156-580-6 (soft cover)
ISBN 978-1-64156-697-1 (e-Book)
Library of Congress Control Number: 2018930482

Printed in the United States of America, North Mankato, Minnesota